The Organized FASHION DESIGNER

by Esther Melander

The forms presented here are copyrighted. You may use, make copies and adapt these forms as needed. These forms cannot be sold individually or as a group.

These and similar forms have been used by me in a business setting. As I have no control on your use of these forms, no warranty or guarantee of any result is provided.

Parking Orbit Publishing
PO Box 6
Soda Springs, ID 83276

ISBN 978-0-98272-451-4

Table of Contents

Introduction

A fashion designer's workspace can be a source of constant inspiration. Fabric swatches, trims, sketches, and art supplies usually abound. This is surrounded by more fabric, thread, sewing machines, computers, and paperwork. Don't forget the rulers, patterns, dress form, scissors, pins, and tape measures. What could be an energized and engaging workspace quickly turns into a cluttered and chaotic space. In order for a designer to turn their love of fashion into a successful business, a designer must find a sense of organization among the chaos.

It is possible to catalog and track of all the details needed to run a design entrepreneur's business. Starting from the early design phase all the way through production you can create a simple file system that will lead you to success. Over the years I have created various forms and filing systems to keep track of all those essential bits of information. I have kept track of information using just a paper file system and electronically with spreadsheets. I have even used pricey commercial software packages designed to keep track of everything in sophisticated databases. At the end of the day though, pencil and paper is the simplest and least expensive system to start and maintain.

Tech Pack

One of the most important, and difficult tasks, for designers is to create a tech pack. A tech pack is a technical design package, or a collection of design specifications needed for manufacturing. A tech pack may be called other names – product package or design specs, just as an example. Regardless, the tech pack is vital to a business as it contains all of the necessary bits of information that a contract or in-house sewing facility needs to know in order to produce your design. It can also be the place that you store all of your cost analysis and sourcing information for each style. This allows you to create a library of designs for future reference.

The forms included in this manual can be used to create a simplified tech pack. If you create a complicated product, you may need a more detailed tech pack that is professionally prepared by a technical designer. A simple tech pack can also help those just starting out in the sewn product industry or even advanced home hobbyists. Detailed explanations follow so that you will know how to fill out each form. Some forms are meant for your own use and some are intended for use by contractors. You may find you will not need all of these forms, so feel free to select the ones that are the most helpful.

A tech pack is always associated with a sample. A sewn sample should be tagged with the style number and hung. The tech pack's paperwork can be organized into notebooks or vertical files by style numbers. Designers can then look through the hanging samples or notebooks to look back at successful or not so successful styles that can be reused or reworked. By having the samples labeled and the paperwork properly filed, it's a simple matter to pull things together to send off to a pattern maker or contractor.

In-house Organization

There are many other details to keep track of and this could include general body measurements and grade rules, cutting guides, style number tracking, and quality specifications. This is the kind of information you want to keep handy when you are drafting a new pattern, measuring a model or talking to your contractor.

Additional forms are included to help organize other aspects of your business. Keeping track of fabric swatches, order processing and fulfillment, and inventory are just a few of the bits of information that is necessary. The only way to free your mind for the fun and creative side of the business is to keep everything else organized.

Book Organization

The book is organized in two parts. The first part contains instructional guides and examples. The second part contains the blank forms. Both sections are organized alphabetically for easy reference.

The forms presented here are copyrighted. You may use, make copies and adapt these forms as needed. These forms cannot be sold individually or as a group. These and similar forms have been used by me in a business setting. As I have no control on your use of these forms, no warranty or guarantee of any result is provided.

You can pick and choose which forms you use and how you use them. The next page contains examples of how and when you might use them.

Forms that can be a part of a simple in-house tech pack
Style sheet with cutting spec
Cost analysis
Finished pattern measurements and drawings
Sewing instructions

Forms for in-house use
Style number tracking
Pattern number tracking
New product tracking
Cost analysis
Inventory
Order processing tracking
Body measurements
Grade rules
Pattern piece catalog
Fabric/trim header
Fabric/trim form

Forms for contractor use
Style sheet with cutting spec
Finished pattern measurements
Sewing instructions

Guides

Body Measurements

This form can be used in a few different ways. First, this form can be used to measure models and dress forms. It can also be used if you choose to do your own measurement study giving you a place to collect data. Finally, this form can be used for body measurements which are the standard body measurements used for your product. It would be helpful to refer to a pattern making manual or purchased measurement specification on how to take these measurements.

Body Measurements

	Size (in inches)			4	5	6	6y		
1	Chest			23	24	25	25.5		
3	Waist			21.5	22	22.5	23		
4	Hip			23.5	24.5	25.5	26.5		
5	Vertical Trunk			39	41	43	44.5		
6	Thigh								

These measurements came from withdrawn body measurement standard for children, CS151-150.

Cost Analysis

This form is used to help you determine the wholesale and/or retail price of your item as well as profitability. If selling wholesale, it is helpful to keep in mind the eventual retail price of your item. This can be written to the side of the wholesale price. Every single item used to make your product needs to be included or else you will lose money. This includes hang tags, labels, shipping boxes, and hangers. Thread is sometimes included in the trims area especially if it is a specialty thread or an especially large quantity is used.

Record each item used in the appropriate table. Multiply the price with the quantity to arrive at the total unit amount. Add the total column to arrive at the Materials total.

Labor charge – the cost per unit to produce a style.

Sale price – The wholesale or retail price for one unit. The sale price is some multiple of the labor and material charges. The exact number depends on your niche, customer expectations, and what the market will bear. Begin by at least doubling the labor + material costs. As you work through this worksheet, the sale price may end up much higher than you expect to cover all of your expenses and still make a profit.

Commission – Money paid to sales representatives and/or online merchant processing fees. This is usually a percentage of the sale price.

Gross = Sale Price – (Labor + Materials + Commission). This is the amount of money you have to pay wages, including yourself, overhead expenses, and saving for future expenses. There should be some money left over for profit too!

Example:
Labor = $20.00
Materials = $30.00
Total Labor + Materials = $50.00
Sale Price = $150.00
Commission (20%) = $150.00 X 0.20 = 30.00
Gross = $150 - ($50.00 + $30.00) = $70.00

Cost Analysis

Style #   21100   **Sample size**   12M

Fabric

Source	Description	Color	Price	Unit	Quantity	Total
Cplus	100 C pink polka dot	pink/wht	4.50	yd	1.25	$5.63
Cplus	100 C broadcloth	pink	3.75	yd	0.25	$0.94

Fabric Total $6.56

Trims, Packaging, Labels

Source	Description	Color	Price	Unit	Quantity	Total
Buttonit	2 hole, 1/2" button	clear	0.01	ea	3	$0.03
Gribbons	French ribbon rose on pin	Dk. Pink	1.00	ea	1.25	$1.25
Gribbons	2" satin ribbon	White	0.63	yd	0.25	$0.16
HangIt	10" hanger	white	1.00	ea	0.10	$0.10
	brand label		0.20	ea	1.00	$0.20
	hang tag		0.15	ea	1.00	$0.15

Trims Total $1.89

Labor $20.00   **Sale Price** $75.00   **Gross** $31.55

Fabric + Trim $8.45   **Commission** $15.00

Total Labor + Materials $28.45

Notes

Pink polka dot fabric has limited availability.
requires 100 yard minimum order

Fabric or Trim Swatch Headers and Forms

A swatch library is essential for a designer. Swatches can be organized in several ways including by style or type which makes it easier to develop ideas. I've included two swatch header sizes and a form. The headers are printed on card stock, folded in half, stapled to the swatch and hole-punched. Headers can be placed on book rings and hung from hooks. The form can be hole-punched and placed in binders. Regardless, it is a good idea to immediately cut a swatch of any fabric or trim upon receipt and inspection and file it with important identifying information and details.

An example of how to organize fabric and trim swatches.

Finished Pattern Measurements

This form is used during production for quality checking. POM stands for point of measure in the first column. The second is a description, such as *Center front neck to hem*. The third column TOL +/-, represents the tolerance or the degree of allowance that a measurement is allowed to vary. For example a t-shirt measurement from the high point of the shoulder to the hem may have a one inch tolerance in which the measurement may be one inch larger or smaller than specified. Be sure to indicate whether a circumference measurement is meant to be taken as the full circumference or half. An example of this would be taking the sleeve or hem circumference of a t-shirt that is laying flat. The remaining columns are for the measurement of each size at that point. Begin by measuring the patterns for the sample size minus the seam allowances. Calculate the remaining sizes by using the grade rules chart. This chart should always be accompanied by a diagram identifying the POM's.

Finished Pattern Measurements

Style: 22250

POM	Size (in inches)	TOL +/-		S	M	L			
1	Center front neck to hem	1		18.25	19.25	20.25			
3	HPS to hem	1		23.5	24.25	25			
4	Across shoulder	0.75		13	13.5	13.75			
5	Across chest	0.75		16.5	17.5	18.5			
6	Sleeve cuff circumference	0.5		13.5	14	14.5			
7	Center back neck to hem	1		22	22.75	23.5			
8	Across back	0.75		16.5	17.5	18.5			
9	Shirt hem circ. (½ measure)	0.75		18	19	20			

The measurements and tolerances in the chart above are made up for this example and do not include all the possible measurements.

Finished Pattern Measurement Drawings   Style # 22250

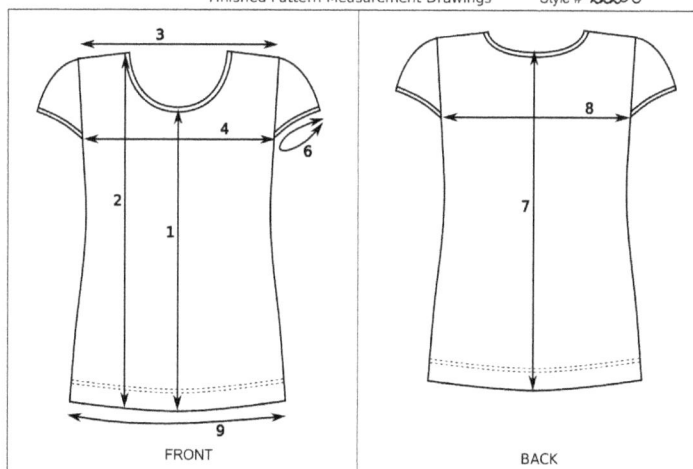

FRONT   BACK

Grade Rules

This form will help you generate a set of basic grade rules. Grade rules are developed from body measurements. You will need a completed Body Measurement Chart or have purchased standard body measurement specifications in order to fill out this chart.

The grade rules entered into this chart will represent the total measurement change for a given measurement. This chart is usually sufficient enough for a professional grader to work out the details. The grade rules can be further broken down to the amount of change at any given point on a pattern piece. How far to break down the grade rules depends on your grader, their mode of practice, and whether they grade by hand or computer.

Example:
1. Begin by indicating your sample size. Enter the number zero down the entire column for your sample size.
2. Substract neighboring measurements and enter the difference. In the example below, substract the size 5 chest measurement from the size 4 chest measurement. The difference is 1 inch. This grade rule says that a size 4 chest measurement is 1 inch smaller than a size 5.

Notice that the grade rule for a size 4 does not have a negative or minus sign before the number 1. Professional graders sometimes drop this notation because it is assumed that sizes to the left of the sample size become smaller and sizes to the right become larger. The extra notation just gets in the way.

Body Measurements

	Size (in inches)			4	5	6	6½		
1	Chest			23	24	25	25.5		
3	Waist			21.5	22	22.5	23		
4	Hip			23.5	24.5	25.5	26.5		
5	Vertical Trunk			39	41	43	44.5		
6	Thigh								

Grade Rules

	Size (in inches)				Sample 5	6	6½		
1	Chest				1 0				
3	Waist				0				
4	Hip				0				

3. Continue to subtract neighboring measurements. In this example, subtract size 5 from size 6 and size 6 from the size 6x.

Body Measurements

	Size (in inches)			4	5	6	6x		
1	Chest			23	(24)	(25)	25.5		
3	Waist			21.5	22	22.5	23		
4	Hip			23.5	24.5	25.5	26.5		
5	Vertical Trunk			39	41	43	44.5		
6	Thigh								

Grade Rules

Sample

	Size (in inches)			4	5	6	6x		
1	Chest			1	0	(1)			
3	Waist				0				
					0				

4. Repeat these steps for each measurement, filling each row by subtracting neighboring measurements.

Body Measurements

	Size (in inches)			4	5	6	6x		
1	Chest			23	24	(25)	(25.5)		
3	Waist			21.5	22	22.5	23		
4	Hip			23.5	24.5	25.5	26.5		
5	Vertical Trunk			39	41	43	44.5		
6	Thigh								

Grade Rules

Sample

	Size (in inches)			4	5	6	6x		
1	Chest			1	0	1	(0.5)		
3	Waist				0				
4	Hip				0				

Inventory

Any business in the United States that manufactures and sells product must keep an inventory for tax purposes. You will need an inventory of finished goods and raw materials in which you assign a dollar amount to the value of those goods. The year will start with a certain amount and end with another. These forms will help you keep track at the beginning and end of the year, though you could take inventories more frequently or as needed during the year. Consult a tax professional for more information on what inventory keeping your specific business needs. Another advantage of tracking inventory is that you will be able to see which styles are selling and thus make decisions on what styles should continue forward.

Product Inventory

List the items placed into inventory for retail and/or wholesale sales by date. Each size and color combination should be listed on a separate line. The final column, Sold, would be the date the item has sold out. Multiply the Quantity column by the Cost column to come up with the Total Cost. Add up the Total Cost column to arrive at a final Total Inventory Cost.

Product Inventory

Opening Date:
Closing Date:

Date in Store	Style #	Name/Description	Color	Size	Quantity	Cost	Total Cost	Sold
04/02/13	12345	Polka dot dress	pink	6M	10	$15.50	$155.00	
04/02/13	12345	Polka dot dress	pink	9M	10	$15.50	$155.00	
04/02/13	12345	Polka dot dress	pink	12M	10	$15.50	$155.00	
04/15/13	12346	Sleeveless dress w/belt	yellow	12M	10	$20.00	$200.00	
04/15/13	12346	Sleeveless dress w/belt	yellow	18M	10	$20.00	$200.00	
04/15/13	12346	Sleeveless dress w/belt	yellow	24M	10	$20.00	$200.00	

Raw Materials Inventory

Keep track of raw materials by listing them by source, or company name. Record the part or style number supplied by the company. Each style and color combination is listed separately. Multiply the Cost column by the Quantity column to arrive at the Total Cost for that raw material item. Add up the entire Total Cost column to arrive at the Total Raw Materials cost.

The Raw Materials Inventory has additional advantages. This form supplies the data needed to complete the Cost Analysis form. Regular raw materials inventories will pin point when to purchase additional supplies or whether some supplies are stagnating and should be sold.

Raw Material Inventory

Opening Date:
Closing Date:

Source	Style #	Name/Description	Color	Cost	Quantity	Unit	Total Cost	
ABC Trim	RB123	5/8" satin ribbon	Pink 1123	0.5	144	yd	$72.00	
ABC Trim	FLO45	Ribbon flower	pnk/moss	0.15	144	ea	$21.60	
Lacey	V345	2" single edge Venice lace	white	3.00	50	yd	$150.00	
Hang It	DL67	10 inch frame hanger	white	1.50	144	ea	$216.00	

New Product Tracking

As a design assistant, it's easy to become overwhelmed in a design meeting at the start of a new season with ideas flown around randomly. I created this form years ago to help me keep track of new styles as they worked their way through the product development process. I was able to use this form whenever upper management wanted to know the status of a particular design. I even used this form in my own business to keep me on task. Place the start date in the left most column and assign a style number using the style number tracking form. As each task is completed, place the date or a check mark in the appropriate column.

New Product Tracking

Date	Style #	Description	Patterns	Cutting Spec	Sample	Cost Analysis	Approval	Photo	Tech Package	Salesmen Samples	Grading		
04/03/13	12345	Pink polka dot dress w/ribbon at waist and ribbon flowers	4/5	4/5	4/7	4/8	4/8	4/9					
04/03/13	12346	Yellow sleeveless sun dress with ribbon belt	4/5	4/5	4/7	4/8							
04/03/13	12347	Lace dress. Venice lace trim. ribbon flower pin	4/5	4/5	4/7	4/8				Canceled too expensive			

Order Process Tracking

Use this form when processing wholesale or retail customer orders. As each task is completed either enter a check mark or date. This form is used in addition to a purchase order and invoice to keep track of the things that can get lost in the shuffle.

Product Ordered - a brief description, style number, and size info. Exact order details will be on the purchase order and/or invoice.

Verify Customer - this includes checking shipping/billing address and phone number, purchasing qualifications, etc.

Inspect Product - The final quality control check before packing the product in a box.

Hang tag, pack product, returns notice - items and steps required in boxing up the product prior to shipping.

Ship - the date the items were picked up by the shipping company

Record payment - logging the payment information into accounting software or ledger

Notify customer - a shipping notice sent to the customer via email or telephone.

Order Process Tracking

Date	PO#	Customer Name	Product Ordered	Quantity Ordered	Print Invoice	Verify Customer	Pull Product	Inspect Product	Hang tags	Pack Product	Returns Notice	Collect Payment	Ship	Record Payment	Notify Customer
04/15	1234	Bella's Boutique	Style 21234, size 3-6-9	12	X	X	X	X	X	X	X	X	04/16		
04/15	1234	Sofie's Baby	Style 21234, size 3-6-9	12	X	X	X	X	X	X	X	X	04/16		
04/15	1234	Dress it up	Style 21234, size 3-6-9	12	X	X	X	X	X	X	X	X	04/16		

Pattern Number Tracking

Pattern makers prefer to assign their own numbers to pattern pieces. This form is provided to track the numbers as they are used. A separate column is included to record the associated style numbers. Pattern numbers are sometimes preceded with the letters PN to indicate a piece or part number. The pattern numbers are assigned sequentially. The description should use common terms like collar, or sleeve cuff and From #'s (see the glossary). More detailed information is recorded in the Pattern Piece Catalog. Pattern numbers should be at least four digits.

The beauty of this kind of system is that the pieces have a reference to a style and parent pieces. The pieces can be used interchangeably or as the base for new styles. It will save your business money to use what you have already created.

As an alternate practice, some pattern makers assign piece numbers that are derived from the style number with a hyphenated letter extension. In this case, this form is not necessary. A list should be created that identifies what the letter extensions represent. This kind of system only works with simple styles that do not have a large number of pieces. This kind of system may not work well with foreign contractors not familiar with English.

Example:
21204-FR
21204-BK
21204-CO

FR = Front
BK = Back
CO = Collar

Pattern Number Tracking

Pattern #	Style #	Description
1001	12345	Basic front bodice with jewel neck
1002	12345	Basic back bodice, button back closure, use with lining

Pattern Piece Catalog

The pattern piece catalog forms come one of two ways. Which form you use depends on your work method or organization style. The first is a form that can be hole-punched and placed in a three ring binder. The second can be printed onto card stock, cut apart and used in a card file. The purpose of this form is so that you can reuse pattern pieces in new styles. Having detailed notes and a simple sketch will help you know how a piece was used.

If you derive new patterns from existing patterns and styles, be sure to note this for future use.

Pattern Piece Catalog

Category: Bodices

Pattern #	From #/Style #	Description	Drawing
1001	12345	Basic front bodice. jewel neck. 3/8" seam allowances. 1/4" seam allowance at neck. Use with 1002 back bodice.	
1002	12345	Basic back bodice. 1/2" extension at center back for button closure. 3/8" seam allowances. 1/4" seam allowance at neck. Use with 1001 front bodice	

Pattern # 1001   Category: Bodices

From #   Style # 1234

Description: Drawing:

Basic front bodice. Jewel neck. 3/8" seam allowances. 1/4" seam allowance at neck. Use with 1002 back bodice

Sewing Instructions

This form provides instructions to sewing machine operators and sewing contractors on how to sew your product. It also helps you determine what machines are required to sew your product.

The seam allowance and seam type columns tell the operator how that sewing step should be executed. Stitch and seam types have been standardized in ASTM D6193. This standard contains approved abbreviations and stitch class types. It is important to refer to this standard when filling out this form.

The details column contains simple descriptions of that sewing step such as, "Seam shoulders." It is not necessary to provide lengthy descriptions. You can also specify stitch type in this area.

The technical drawings include both a front and back view of your product. Add callouts for each seam indicating the seam allowance and type as needed. For more complex products, an additional sewing instruction form minus the drawing boxes is included.

Sewing Instructions

Style # _____ 21100

Technical Sketch

Front	Back

Step	Seam Allowance	Seam Type	Details
1	3/8"	SSa-1	Seam shoulders of shell
2	3/8"	SSa-1	Seam shoulders of lining
3	1/4"	SSa-1	Seam lining to shell at center back, neck, and armholes.
4			turn out, press

Style Number Tracking

A style number is a series of numbers assigned to styles as they are developed. Style numbers, rather than names, are easier to write on forms and samples, makes you look more professional, and is easier to track. The style number becomes the key organizational point for every piece of paperwork related to your design, from the initial design phase all the way through order writing with a retailer. Numbers should be used sequentially. A log to keep track of them is a very useful reference that helps to avoid accidentally assigning two numbers to the same style or two styles with the same number.

A style number can be encoded so that anyone in your business can know what the style is supposed to be by merely looking at the number. A style number code is unique to each business. The formula for the style number code should be written at the top of the log so that you know how to create new numbers in the future. The example below can be adapted to create your own formula to suit your own needs. Try to anticipate everything you hope to do in the future even if you only focus on one area now. Not all information related to the style should be encoded. For example, it's not necessary to encode short or long sleeves or color information here.

Guidelines
1. Numbers should be used sequentially
2. Numbers should be at least five digits
3. Do not encode too many details
4. Plan for future growth

Example:
Style number consists of 5 digits

Style Number Tracking

Formula: First number 1=Boy, 2=Girl; Second number 1=Dress, 2=Top, 3=Pants
Last three numbers = Style Number

Style #	Description
21100	Girl's dress, pink polka dot fabric, ribbon flowers at waist
21101	Girl's yellow dress, ribbon belt, flower pin

Style Sheet and Cutting Spec

A combination style sheet and cutting spec is an attempt to save paperwork. Traditionally, the cutting spec, also called a cutter's must or pattern card, is printed on heavy card stock and pinned to a sample. By combining the cutting spec with the style sheet, the paperwork can travel from the pattern maker to the sample maker without interruption. Simply fold the form in half and pin it to the sample. Once the style is approved, a copy of this form can be hole-punched or slipped into a protective sleeve and put into a style file.

Fill out the areas that are necessary for your business.

Size scale - the size range, such as Junior, Infant, or Toddler. It can be expressed by a combination of words and numbers, such as Missy 6-8-10-12-14. It may also be helpful to note the sample size.

From # - If a new style is a derivation of a previous style, then note the style number of the previous style.

The technical sketch does not have to be fancy. Be sure to indicate any important style details and construction notes with callouts.

The table below the cutting spec is intended for fabric information. List the fabrics using letter designations starting with the dominant fabric. The letter designations are then used in the cutting spec in the Fabric column. The letters are also used on the technical sketch to indicate where fabrics are used in the design.

Cutting Spec

Cut	Fabric	Description	Pattern #
1	AB	Bodice front	1001
2	AB	Bodice back	1002
1	A	Skirt front	1003
2	A	Skirt back	1004

	Source		Fabric width/notes
A	Cplus	Pink Polka Dot	45
B	Cplus	Solid Pink	45

Cutting Spec

Cut	Fabric	Description	Pattern #
1	AB	Bodice front	1001
2	AB	Bodice back	1002
1	A	Skirt front	1003
2	A	Skirt back	1004

Source		Description	Fabric width/notes
A	Cplus	Pink Polka Dot	45
B	Cplus	Solid Pink	45

Notes:

Style Sheet

Date: 4/1/13

Style No. 21100

Web Name/Title: Dottie

Season: Spring 2013

From No.

Size Scale: Infant Sample 12 M

Description:

Technical Sketch/Swatches

Pillow rose pin

2 inch Satin Ribbon

2 inch Blind hem

Cut shell out of A
Cut lining of B

Glossary

Callouts – Additional information on a sketch indicated with a line or arrow that points to the relevant area.

Cutter's must – Another term for a cutting specification.

From # - The style number or pattern number from which a new style or pattern piece is derived.

POM - Acronym for point of measure. Indicates the area to be measured on a drawing.

Size scale - The size range, such as Junior, Infant, or Toddler. It can be expressed by a combination of words and numbers, such as Missy 6-8-10-12-14. It may also be helpful to note the sample size.

Style number - A series of numbers assigned to styles as they are developed

Tech pack - A combination of paper work and product sample that provides information needed for manufacturing.

Tolerance - The degree of allowance that a measurement is allowed to vary.

Resources

Sewing and Pattern making supplies
South Star Supply - southstarsupply.com
Wawak - wawak.com
Sew True - sewtrue.com

Measurement and Spec Info
ASTM - http://webstore.ansi.org/
Search for these standards:
D4910 – Size standard for infants, sizes preemie-24M
D5219 – Terminology for body dimensions and apparel sizing
D5585 – Size standard for Women, Misses figure type, sizes 2-20
D5586 – Size standard for Women, aged 55+
D6240 – Size standard for Men, sizes 34-60 (Regular)
D6860 – Size standard for Boys, sizes 6-24, Husky
D6192 – Size standard for Girls, sizes 2-20 (Reg & Slim), plus sizes
D6193 – Standard practice for stitches and seams
D6829 – Size standard for Juniors, size 0-19

Free measurement charts
(These are withdrawn standards available in the public domain. The web addresses for these are constantly changing, so do a google search. Keep in mind these standards are out of date).
CS151-50 – Children
PS42-70 – Women
PS45-71 – Young Men
PS36-70 – Boys
PS54-72 – Girls

Useful websites
Fashion-incubator.com
patternschool.com
designloft.blogspot.com

Useful books
Aldrich, Winifred. Metric pattern cutting for children's wear and baby wear, 2009.
Armstrong, Helen Joseph. Patternmaking for fashion design, 2009.
Fasanella, Kathleen. The entrepreneur's guide to sewn product manufacturing, 1995.
Handford, Jack. Professional pattern grading for women's, men's, and children's apparel, 2003.

Blank Forms

Body Measurements

	Size (in)								
1	Chest								
3	Waist								
4	Hip								
5	Vertical Trunk								
6	Thigh								
7	Neck base								
8	Armscye								
9	Upper arm girth								
10	Cross-back width								
11	Shoulder length								
12	Scye depth								
13	Total crotch length								
14	Shoulder and arm length								
15	Head and neck length								
16	Cervical height								
17	Cervical to knee								
18	Cervical to waist								
19	Waist height								
20	Waist to knee								
21	Waist to hip								
22	Crotch height								
23	Knee height								
24	Ankle height								

Cost Analysis

Style # _____   Sample size _____

Fabric

Source	Description	Color	Price	Unit	Quantity	Total

Fabric Total _____

Trims, Packaging, Labels

Source	Description	Color	Price	Unit	Quantity	Total

Trims Total _____

Labor _____   Sale Price _____   Gross _____

Fabric + Trim _____   Commission _____

Total Labor + Materials _____

Notes

Fabric Header - Small

Source:
Style:
Color:
Width:
Origin:
Content:
Price:

Source:
Style:
Color:
Width:
Origin:
Content:
Price:

Source:
Style:
Color:
Width:
Origin:
Content:
Price:

Source:
Style:
Color:
Width:
Origin:
Content:
Price:

Source:
Style:
Color:
Width:
Origin:
Content:
Price:

Source:
Style:
Color:
Width:
Origin:
Content:
Price:

Fabric Header - Large

Source:

Style:

Color:

Width:

Content:

Origin:

Price:

Source:

Style:

Color:

Width:

Content:

Origin:

Price:

Finished Pattern Measurements

Style:

POM	Size (in)	TOL +/-							
1									
3									
4									
5									
6									
7									
8									
9									
10									
11									
12									
13									
14									
15									
16									
17									
18									
19									
20									
21									
22									
23									
24									

Finished Pattern Measurement Drawings   Style #

FRONT

BACK

Grade Rules

Sample

	Size (in)								
1	Chest				0				
3	Waist				0				
4	Hip				0				
5	Vertical Trunk				0				
6	Thigh				0				
7	Neck base				0				
8	Armscye				0				
9	Upper arm girth				0				
10	Cross-back width				0				
11	Shoulder length				0				
12	Scye depth				0				
13	Total crotch length				0				
14	Shoulder and arm length				0				
15	Head and neck length				0				
16	Cervical height				0				
17	Cervical to knee				0				
18	Cervical to waist				0				
19	Waist height				0				
20	Waist to knee				0				
21	Waist to hip				0				
22	Crotch height				0				
23	Knee height				0				
24	Ankle height				0				

Date	Style #	Description																				
		Patterns																				
		Cutting Spec																				
		Sample																				
		Cost Analysis																				
		Approval																				
		Photo																				
		Tech Package																				
		Salesmen Samples																				
		Grading																				

New Product Tracking

Order Process Tracking

Date	PO#	Customer Name	Product Ordered	Quantity Ordered	Print Invoice	Verify Customer	Pull Product	Inspect Product	Hang tags	Pack Product	Returns Notice	Collect Payment	Ship	Record Payment	Notify Customer	

Pattern Number Tracking

Pattern #	Style #	Description

Pattern Piece Catalog

Category:

Pattern #	From #/Style #	Description	Drawing

Pattern #   Category:

From #   Style #

Description: Drawing:

Pattern #   Category:

From #   Style #

Description: Drawing:

Pattern #   Category:

From #   Style #

Description: Drawing:

Product Inventory

Opening Date:
Closing Date:

Date in Store	Style #	Name/Description	Color	Size	Quantity	Cost	Total Cost	Sold

Raw Material Inventory

Opening Date:
Closing Date:

Source	Style #	Name/Description	Color	Cost	Quantity	Unit	Total Cost	

Sewing Instructions

Style # _____

Technical Sketch

Front	Back

Step	Seam Allowance	Seam Type	Details

Sewing Instructions

Style # _____

Step	Seam Allowance	Seam Type	Details

Style Number Tracking

Formula:

Style #	Description

Style Sheet

Date:

Style No.

Web Name/Title:

Season:

From No.

Size Scale

Description:

Description:

Technical Sketch/Swatches

Cutting Spec

Cut	Fabric	Description	Pattern #

Source	Fabric width/notes

Notes:

Trim Catalog

Category:

Source:	
Style:	
Color:	
Width:	
Content:	
Origin:	
Price:	

Source:	
Style:	
Color:	
Width:	
Content:	
Origin:	
Price:	

Source:	
Style:	
Color:	
Width:	
Content:	
Origin:	
Price:	

Source:	
Style:	
Color:	
Width:	
Content:	
Origin:	
Price:	

Source:	
Style:	
Color:	
Width:	
Content:	
Origin:	
Price:	

Esther is a 16 year veteran of the fashion industry specializing in children's special occasion clothing. She has been involved with the manufacturing and selling of children's clothing in big box retail and specialty boutique stores as a pattern maker, grader, and technical designer. Currently, Esther blogs about technical aspects of the fashion industry and works as a part-time librarian. Esther's blog features an exploration of children's clothing design, the book arts, gluten free baking, knitting, and whatever else she's working on at the moment.

You can read Esther's blog and contact her at www.designloft.blogspot.com.

www.ingramcontent.com/pod-product-compliance
Lightning Source LLC
LaVergne TN
LVHW081322060426
835509LV00015B/1635